Man Moon Earth

Prithvindra Chakravarti

Man   Moon   Earth

For
Ulli and Georgina Beier

Man Moon Earth
ISBN 978 1 74027 552 1
Copyright © text Jayasri Chakravarti 2009

First published 2009
Reprinted 2016

GINNINDERRA PRESS
PO Box 3461 Port Adelaide 5015
www.ginninderrapress.com.au

Contents

Echoes & Images	7
The Jintipirri and I	9
We All Discard Our Eyes	11
Twin Mangoes	12
The Visitant	13
Breadfruit	14
Biography of an Ex-gangleader	15
A Kaugere Tale	17
The Lavara and His Children	19
Too Simple?	20
Man Moon Earth	21
A Trilogy	23
Return of the Sprouting Skull	24
Mosquito	30
Ants	31
Buffalo	32
You	33
She	34
She Again	35
Theatre of Skills	36
Monglu	37
Scrolls & Clippings	39
Joyride	41
In My Rainbow Billabong	42
The Earth Cracked	43
The Majestic Standstill	44
Kookaburra's Laugh	45
The Knight Errant	46
Passage of Fire	47

The Day	48
An Idler's World Cup 2002	49
Gujarat 2002	50
Sporting Over	51
The Quest	52
A Dazzling Trek	53
A Deafening Hug	54
The Journey	55
The Amazing Grace	56
Fraternity Meal	57
The Grand Wushi Ware	58
The Gecko	59
A Slight Tremor	60
The Haze	61
Peace	62
Bali 2002	63
The Caterpillar	65
Kunabibi	66
The Arc	67
The Summit	68
About the Author	72

Echoes & Images

The Jintipirri and I

The little jintipirri
Shrugged off the dew.
While pacing up and down
In my moist intimate yard
She shook off the rest
From her dishevelled feathers.
I knew instantly
What was awaiting me
This day
In the knotted world.

She paused
Wagged her tail
Pecked at titbits
And poured her warmth
Profusely –
The giggling buoyant figurines
The intricate handiwork
The wriggling plaited shadows
Drowning the whole surface.
Unmoved
I overtook her.

She flew desperately to a poinciana
Near the edge
Washed in the dawn's cool glow –
Her amber eyes
Gazing at the far horizon
Her chattering mouth
Cracking riddles.
Standing still
I simply startled her
With my piercing silence.

Flapping the motifed wings
Vigorously
She took off
For the last time
Carving a crescent in the air
To reap a glorious bloom
And sat at ease
On the crest
Of a lightning-struck palm tree
By the creek.
But I perching firm
On the veranda of my cottage
Outmanoeuvred her again

By prevailing upon the immense expanse
She wove around her
So diligently.

Jintipirri is willy wagtail in Warumungu, a central Australian language in the Tennant Creek region.

We All Discard Our Eyes

We all discard our eyes one day.
Sticking them on the wall, we scratch around
Caught in a cobweb, relishing our rest peacefully.
Once Anancy created a whole world,

Now he will undo his mischief, relieving us
Of our routine: no more seeing then
Those soft and harsh colours, figurines, ribs –
Only sticky gum will put us together

If we fall apart. We will enjoy the warmth
Released by the dazzling gazes disowned long before.

Twin Mangoes

We never spoke, never sat face to face.
Our company evaporated with the morning dew.
The midday sweat dried on the quilted
Rice field: our worn-out scarves and robes

Reincarnated in the embroidery – the ripples
All around, a blossom in the centre,
The rainbow snakes guarding the borders.
We never sat face to face, never spoke.

We hung like twin mangoes
From the forked bough of an ancient tree.

The Visitant

Under the misty canopy
The untamed stem
In the crimson vase
Wears a hundred petals:

Dreams play briskly
In the quivering waters
Pushing all the sands
Towards the edge.

A beaming face
Sails like a moon
In the clear sky
Beneath the turbulent sea.

The unuttered words
Reluctantly melt away
In the radiant lotus
Utterly entwined

In the crystal vase
Stirring the visiting
Unbending stem
Deep into the bottom.

Breadfruit

Two breadfruit are hanging from a bough
In my grandmother's abandoned backyard.
The lumps travel in the air back and forth
Colliding routinely: tip tap teep taep teep taep.

No two eyes collide with each other,
A fair distance in between they manage
To meet at a point on lumps, figures,
And action-packed memorable events.

The breadfruit are no eyes, they don't
Ever travel beyond a certain point,
Never able to reach any ludicrous lumps,
Fanciful figures or adventurous actions

For they are amorous lumps themselves
Hankering after each other, cast into
Large round figures, dangling in glee
For the only action of a premeditated collusion.

Hidden under the rough greenish crocodile skin
The creamy flesh gets stirred by the itchy tail
Pushing them to a scratching field – an ensemble
Of actions, figure hunting and lump tracking.

Biography of an Ex-gangleader

Tapei the ex-gangleader of the flying fox clan
Pats a fat cockroach
– His only companion this morning
Seated on the back of his palm.

'You didn't break and enter
The cupboard last night.
Instead, mowed the crisp, curly gras
That I nurtured on my bigman's head.
With your energy and taste
You could have removed
The packing-box floor
Of my Morata nest.
You've saved me, mate,
From ending up in bankruptcy'.

Stuffed with freshly harvested crop
The ingenious, princely creature
Lazily rests
On the undulating back of Tapei's
Safe, relaxed, palm,
Finds infinite peace
Enjoyed never before.

Finds release
From the daily rounds
For he has planted today
In man
A penetrating spell!

Tapei now strokes his husked coconut crown
With the same hand
That patted a moment ago
The shiny, dark brown back of his saviour.

'You did break and enter
My retreat
And took away my treasures.
You did remove
Those planks that supported my tilting torso.
You've rescued me, mate,
From entering my web again.'

'Gras' is hair in Melanesian Pidgin (Tok Pisin). 'bigman' is a self-made man of a chief's stature in Melanesian tradition. Morata is a squatters' settlement adjacent to the University at Waigani in the National Capital District of Papua New Guinea. It is generally believed to be a nest of criminals.

A Kaugere Tale

After a hard day's work of burning
The rusty, crumbled tin roofs
Of the Kaugere slums –
The sun set exhilaratingly
Behind the hills.

The chick on the floor
For the first time
Breathed a sigh:
His dry mouth gasping for moisture.

The teenage hibiscus-feathered mother
After a hard day's courage
Of pleasing the cranky typewriter
In a Hohola garage
Nestled in her boss's shed
Drooped over her dream
Thrusting her two unripe pawpaws
Alternately
Into the tiny mouth.
The baby giggled:
The winking eyes peeped through the torn blouse
At those chattering skinny shadows
Who gave him company in the day's exile.

The untied hen had a rough ride
In a rattling ute turned into a PMV.
But, neatly tidying her hair
And securely tucking the Taiwan-made skirt –
She pulled her unfailing bones
To light the pit stove in the yard.
The hot sweat rolled
Into the receding tide on her back.
The dented aluminium pot slowly boiled.
And the ancient wrinkled night
Softly sat on the bamboo fence,
Stammered like a baby owl
Sprinkling herbs over the absorbing yarn:
The steam coiling upwards
From the Kaugere earth
Bubbling in delirium.

The Lavara and His Children

Lazily coiling around a rafter under the roof
At the back
The lavara sinks in a purple meditation.
The midday warmth
Seeps through the corrugated quilt.
The slender, disenchanted, diamond-studded slough
Whispers in the cacia branch
Delaying the prized rejuvenation of the reptile.

Boys still dress shabbily.
Girls run astray. And lapuns
Break buai between their bleeding gums.
The souls remain unblessed,
Utterly unenlightened –
Can't recognise the calm hands
Behind the task force gloves,
Can't even decipher the buddhas
In their own little coral crops
Sticking out in shallow inlets.

The lahara wind ejects sighs and hisses.
Holidaying in the safe
Self-distanced, highest elegance
The emancipated lavara fades further
Into his treasured slumber.

Too Simple?

Too simple in shorts and thongs?
The mausgras and knotted hair look too harsh?
Harsher still is his smoked mullet posture?
Is he too feeble to raise fists?
Too cold to fire anger even if we rubbish him?

The shorts and thongs
Flap and clatter
And the knotted locks nod with ease
While the untamed biro
Draws doodles tickling his face.

The morning shower
Drowns his wrinkled ticklings
In a pool of tadpoles
Who lose their tails when the day smiles.
The toads grow robust croaking in bliss.

But he sinks in a quiet brooding
When the fireflies meet in a rendezvous.
His sweat boils and thickens
Treks along those trails
Cut deep into his conscience.

Man Moon Earth

After running over her puppy
My wheels jammed.
The poor creature just fell from the moon's lap.
The screech
Heightening the discordant pitches
Reluctantly faded
Into a series of long winding sighs.
I quietly limped back
To my shell
With my singled-out impolite unshaped soul.

*

The sticky summer's sweat
Softened the dry brittle dough
Of the most remorseful state:
The yolk throbbed –
The blinking blazed with excitement
Melting the iced wrinkles
On my face:
My lonely lawn
Filled with tickling footprints
Only to be robbed next moment
By those two agitated obstinate wings.

I recognised the clean feathers
Neatly combed,
The chubby back
Brightly decorated,
The slender neck
Prudently craned forward
Subduing the gorgeous gem-studded gear.

And I saw
The sun-tanned crown
Above the purple beak
Pointing to the shore,
While driving the starving footprints
Zigzagging the fast widening valleys.

The slimy yellow shallow lagoon
Stretched endlessly.
Coming out of the shell
I perched on a mangrove branch –
My thirst crawling along the trunk
Deep down the roots
Cutting through the flesh
Of the tide-fevered
Bewitching earth.

A Trilogy

Standing on the corpse
Of my conquered leisure
I spoke. She nodded
Adding cadence to my curiosity.

I swayed. She plucked a few
Frangipanis for the scenario.
The ripples awakened
My little lagoon

Where the mud cake churned
Melting in my blood.

Return of the Sprouting Skull

The Sinagu Cliff
Burst into a hilarious shake:
A midget rock with prickly limbs
Long exiled in the grandma's bushland,
Jumped crashing on her lap
Only to roll away
Spinning and bouncing
Down the slope
Reaching the pebbled edge of the Crystal Rapids
Nestled in the valley below.

Well nursed, it wore
A pebble's innocuous face,
Cracking through the jaws
Its slender tongue
Sticking out mumbling.

Out of eyeholes
Sprouted tender shoots
And in a wink exuberated with a profusion of shy
Adze-shaped leaves
Forked upwards upon a tall
Restless trunk
To embrace the feeble sky
Bent with ageing, worrying.

The protracted sleep
In the old disabled mother's legs
Disappeared:
The sands dissolved in the stirred stare.

While the leaves widened
And stretched
And colour changed
Showing their deep vein fatigue
The paired eyes peeped
Through the bushy crown
And the yellow bulges radiated
Throbbed
Rattling vigorously,

And sliding down the smooth slender
Celebrated pole
That bridged the earth
With the fragile sun-soaked
Foliage of the cloudland
Rested comfortably
On the Sinagu's crest.

The throat tickled
And giggled
And joked a lot
Pricking the ancient woman's
Painted fluorescent reminiscences.

I cried, 'Hi, there.'
A nodding blushed
With a tint of modesty.
Pulling courage I pleaded,
'You've sacrificed much for us,
Now come down.
Be with us.'

The tattooed face rolled
Down the slope.
Gathering speed
Suddenly stopped
And twirled
And rolled again.
Finally crouched
Half buried in the innocent ground
Under my feet:
It was the skull –
The same old oval-shaped earthly lump:
Worms in the mouth,
Insects in the eyeholes –
Gaze deep –
Drilling into my guilt.
I shivered like a toad
Before an advancing hungry python.
But he wore a quick polished smile.
'Mi tasol.'

His polite simplicity
Turned into stubbornness
And the stretched look
Shaped into scars of long-forgiven episodes
Smeared with humiliation and occasional
Bloodlettings.
The deep-cut treks of my reverie
Meandered through the undulated offences:
The chronicles pleated into the gorgeous rainbow
Spanning the ever receding horizon
In my mutilated sky.

I surprised him by pulling an enormous catapult.
The sky shattered
Littering the whole valley.
But emerged again
With the gnawing teeth protruding at me.
I gave him – quick
A massive bloodshot kick
With all my flesh-born force.
My blood reddened
As his arrogance thickened
On his mute jaws
Which promptly clammed my foot
With great velocity
And dragged me over the rough, rocky,
Bushy cliff.
He was climbing up victoriously
While spitting a fiery stare at me
All the while.
I screamed.

The familiar embodiment of jocularity
And ambivalence
Solidly seated on my shoulder
Made faces at him.
The lime-washed nudity
Tightly glued to my indulgence.
While rushing to the top
He picked up his spare limbs
That was awaiting his grace since disowned
By his own ego.

Now grabbing me he challenged,
'What makes you scream?'
And I just boiled again
With unshot screams in my throat.

He discerned a silent, faint trembling
In my gladdened obedience.
My shrill agony made the bony Sinagu shed tears.
Along the wet, slippery track
We struggled for grip
In our own styles,
But, alas, fell down pathetically
To the bottom.
'Let's talk,' he whispered.

Half opening my mouth,
I managed to eject only a grunt.
But he – now in a clear loud voice –
Commanded,
'Put me on your shoulder.'
And I instantly lifted my head
And let it drop below
Bouncing on the ridges –
The inflated ribs of the mourning earth,
And putting on that stubborn skull
On my bleeding conscience,
I resumed the tenuous journey
With perseverance and loyalty.

At last my crude brevity was rewarded.
It joyously brought me to the crest.
Enthroned with rites and pomp
I beheld the vast unabashed valley
Through my newly possessed treasure –
The itchy, enchanting, deeply bored eyeholes
Still infested with dinosaur-aged
Siblings of adventures and refinements.

The moss-engrossed pebble on the bottom
Did radiate for a while
Like the evening lamp in an abandoned shrine.
But the slimy charcoaled green soot pushed it
To the far edge –
The heavy soul-drained lump
Floated in the air
– The swollen, sterile, silted satellite
Shedding its blazing crazes
To cool me down.

Mosquito

In the afternoon
She walks, wanders, and comes and plays:
Sits on my lap, hangs on my shoulder,
Covers my neck with kisses;
Places her nose on my cheek,
Presses and rubs it
        Lovingly.

In the evening
She sings songs, dances wildly;
Engraves her name with teeth…
Scratches and burns my cheeks;
Reaches for my waist with her fingers,
Slackens and unties my robe
        Silently.

In the night
She comes in a swarm, submerges me
And digs a canal with her picks and axes:
The fleet of boats rides on the low tide
And the heavy sediment of salt only sharpens
My anguish and my fever
        Incessantly.

Ants

Bits of flesh in their mouths…
Cheering and thrilling…
They are running, shoulder to shoulder,
In rows, in lines, marching peelpeel peelpeel…

Crossing veranda…
Climbing up walls
Towards an unknown tunnel
In rows, in lines, marching peelpeel peelpeel…

A crow died yesterday…
No trace of it is left now…
And crows have gathered from ten countries
In rows, in lines, marching peelpeel peelpeel…

Draught blown by wings…
Kahkah kahkah by the drumming beaks…
And lumps in their mouths
In rows, in lines, marching peelpeel peelpeel…

They are running in an unending flow…
Cheering and thrilling…
A battalion of ants
In rows, in lines, marching peelpeel peelpeel…

Buffalo

Was it a buffalo that was roaming about?
Spearing the ground with his crooked horns?
Did the hard ground crack?

The scratches resembled a drawing.
Was it an alpona pattern? Or a victory flag? Or a sign
Intended to be somebody's address?

The deep cut lines on the surface rolled into time
Only to fall off again like broken days
Covered with thick dust, the buffalo-headed soul
Dragged the weight of his body, nodding his crooked horns.

You

Your body wrapped in the sun like a sari,
Your hair darkened by the earth's womb,
Your eyes lined by distant shores, shadowed by cloudy afternoons.
Your finger raised against the obstinate presence of time.

Forests tremble, shadows shatter on blunt surfaces,
Doorways shut out the weeping storm; a trap is laid
Drawn with lime on the ground and charged with incantations…
Then soaked red with blood, lumps of straw are stuffed in the hollow figure –

It is you who remains awake through the ages
That have thickened and matted your hair so endearingly.

She

One day, casting her shadow on the water
She stretched her legs on the bank of the lake:
She dipped into the water and cried loudly.
Next day she dried and warmed up her clock.

She looked around, opening her opaque eyes;
The burning sun entered into her bushy hair
And soon slipped away like a frustrated clown.
Opening her toothless mouth she shot a big laughter…

'If the sleep-filled eyes sink deeper into my creased face
I won't even see the clown, the clown, the clown…'

She Again

Building a sandcastle in the bed of a dried-up creek
She wept, filling the moat with tears.
The basketload of hair, heavy with sweat, pressed hard on her head:
The lice, who had been living there for ages, were horrified.

Settling down on the roof of an abandoned house on a market day
She looked below: a juggler was spinning himself on a long bamboo pole…
Suddenly he jumped to the roof and drowned the woman in surprise,
Like a rusty clock, her heart stopped to beat.

Young lice came forth from the eggs that were hidden under knots and dandruff
To meet a battalion of worms on the battlefield of carrion.

Theatre of Skills

Kids of Mohan Bagan Lane talked of Pele decades ago, then of
Maradona, now praising Roberto, Rivaldo, and look for a striker
Of their own to terrorise the bullies, surely for a kill. In the back street
Barricaded with fallen bricks and slabs, the ball roars in full blast

Over dribbling, passing, sliding and lightning shots.
Little Dahlia, from a nearby bustee, cuddles her newest friend –
A cute puppy. Barking deafening notes she seizes her prey
By her tender tail with such an expert skill. A real wizard.

While the soulmates are in a world of bliss, the fans in exasperation
Hit their heads against each other in their makeshift field.

Monglu

A carrying pole on his shoulder, trays dangling
From the two ends – Monglu in his turban returns
From the weekly market – Melu, his granddaughter
Telling stories to her new dolls in the front swing;

Heaps of cargo in the rear, gently swaying
With salt, sugar, spices, tobacco in packets;
Savouries in leaf cups, cheese balls in jars;
A bottle of herbal oil for his ailing aunt.

The mother of six puppies by the side, puffing,
Gallantly brings her master home.

Scrolls & Clippings

Joyride

Frilled leaves of copper
Sail about in a great pomp
In the calm emerald water
Of the Rainbow billabong:

The mist around melting away.
Dragonflies in green attire
Come rushing to the shore
From behind the ridges.

Hijacking the floats in a blitz
They'll pitch a flotilla holiday.

In My Rainbow Billabong

So many seas in my rainbow billabong
Where cockatoos feast on sumptuous lilies
And galahs wait for their lookalikes to echo.
The centre stage is a vast expanse of violet:

Indigo in the bottom. Blue, green, yellow and red
Along the shores. Pale, cloudy, glittery and deep
Orange in the corners. Ripples roll into streamers,
Ruptures into tides, a million moon long voyage

To the beach where hot sands turn into soft petals
To welcome the lubras to fill their coolemons.

The Earth Cracked

At last the scrubs rustled behind the magnetic mounds,
The tall eunuchs, aged purple, still partying, sipping trickles
From the Majesty's goblet. The day was well rewarded,
The thick dust loosened to let the limbs yawn and stretch

In the baked breeze, hairy fingers waving for an ensemble,
Hunchback vines climbing stumps for a glance,
Grubs giggling in excitement in hollow branches,
Hordes of millipedes rumbling under dead leaves.

No luck for the bulging eyes of the guards this millennium
For the earth cracked to adore her mates mute or jovial.

The Majestic Standstill

Lumps of earth, fractured twigs, a twisted plastic comb,
Chewed up leaves in the tongue of a wrinkled bark –
Neatly packed on back, crown towering in the air -
The frill-neck lizard majestically stood on the road.

Aha! The bush is so clean, polished! A straight open cut
Tunnel! No treat, no ware, not even a dead ant to pick -
A barren bazaar! Who comes there! Won't get anything, mate.
It's a damn wacky haunting mortuary without corpses.

Luxury sedans, utes, road trains and the Harley Davidsons
Were all rounded up by his whipping speed-trap sharp gaze.

Kookaburra's Laugh

The kookaburra returned to the shoulder of the wobbly woolly butt,
Watching inquisitively: no, no chicks, not even a fly noticed
Her fall down below, head hitting on the glossy sheet of silver
Making the whole school of plumb jubilant mullets belly dance

With mouths open stuffing thrilling funs into their wriggly guts.
The long shore lined with half raised rods, jackets under hats
Stood on erect logs in the mud, nose pointing to floats, folded
Chairs still left in wraps on the grass. Her throat ballooned

Bursting: don't those blokes ever lean on back? Shouldn't they
Throw their hats at the entertainers? Won't they laugh?

The Knight Errant

The spider trapped a young itinerant ant unaware.
The carcass packed neatly in the silk roll, dangled
Gently, swinging in the cool evening, sweating
In the night's dews, freshening up in the morning sun,

While briskly sprinkling the fragrance of honey,
Oozing from the round belly collapsed long ago.
The maddening sweet breeze thickened around
When the jaws of the knight cut through the roll

To take aim at the next awaiting adventurous errand
Trekking through the rippling razor-edge silver web.

Passage of Fire

After a shower, the valley looked greener.
Dashing out of crevices the ants spread their wings.
A fat one, still in motion, found solace
In my torn sleeve. I welcomed her dearly:

'You've chosen the right spot, but the wrong man, I'm afraid.
I'm about to light a campfire for I'm shivering.'
First the smoke, then a spark. Then the spectacular flames
With tongues pouring saliva of bright orange.

The sky wore a second veil, I my second manhood. My mate
Having quenched her thirst in fire, set off on her second voyage.

The Day

The day broke gallantly, the spirit of liberty sparkling
In the crisp sun, and the sneaky breeze craftily drawing
Doodles on the silky cheeks at workstations. Then the mice
Roared. The steel frame gave in, platinum ribs crackling,

The stars in pale blue looked trillion light years away.
Glitters of towering crowns grudgingly hid under a desert
Of blackened earth, the charred throbbing feet darting
Through the rubbles for light. Screams faded into whispers.

The startled fractured white shadows with shaven heads
Thawed their frozen bones in night's molten tar for a stride.

An Idler's World Cup 2002

Rhinos versus Mosquitoes

The soccer field crackled when the moon landed
On the penalty zone. Rhinos, skin all brown rust,
Feet numbed, stood still, and the netted goalposts
Melted away by the glorious silver glow.

Gathering wings, the Mosquitoes flew abuzz,
Lungs ballooned with the stormy clapping.
Rolling heads returned to their seats. And the eyeballs
Jumping out of the stadium rushed to the arena

For a hot samba. Thick sweating of the battlers darkened
By their heavy breathing on the viewers' screens.

Gujarat 2002

Dug open with bare claws, the pits, large and small,
Flood with molten ruby – the hot pursued treasure
Reaching the deep vaults under the jaunty wings,
The eyebrows greying under the folds of crowns.

Around the banyan tree it all happened not long ago –
Vows exchanged between the turbans and moustaches,
Signs aired auspiciously and the humble fakir tamed
The most monstrous bull on the earth by twisting its tail.

Not by powdered rage. The truth was heard, sanity heeded,
Courage rewarded. But that's past. Witnessing claws again.

Sporting Over

Sporting over, the big-mouths croaked in unison,
And raising their fighting hind legs in triumph, hopped out.
Rose bushes fallen, jasmines smashed, young gardenias
Stripped of virginity – an odorous dump in the outskirt.

Sweating heavily in the ghastly mist, the morning broke, staggering
On the ivory teapoy in my balcony: the breeze wriggled like tinsel,
Jigsawed into creamy, crimson, satin petals, and neatly reshuffled
Into an adorable bouquet, hardening the necks of those acrobats stiff.

Throats ballooned, the amphibious matadors in the swamp
Fumbled terribly to maroon to the other shore.

The Quest

Sometime it's a jingle from upstairs, or a whisper from a distant bush,
Sometime it's a faint ray through a crack, or a crinkled rainbow in a well,
Burrowing into the obstinate dumb metalled blank for a wondrous trek
Spreading unwieldy wings above ridges, under the scorching eyes.

Sometime a mere dot appears, or perhaps an unmarked speck
With a halo around breaking into the space – then a contour,
Then a face, and always a face beaconing dazzling flashes,
The dark rainforest fuelling incessantly the unframed flames

Of my anguish sharpening the quest for that unfathomed
Unbound sea where my etchings must take a solemn dip.

A Dazzling Trek

Straightening her crinkled limbs, the slick green sprout
Craned her way through the charcoal-grey water
Only to fall on the back in the eye shaped lotus pool,
Robust stems gazing in the sheltered audience:

The etching on the muddy bottom was still setting the tale
Of trekking through the ridges and valleys, and ridges
Again, the stretch still untrodden to be a long adventure
In rhymed quatrains and melodious enchanting lyrics.

She came to adore the garden, bubbling with joy, gifting
Away her dazzles – a spark each – to the sinking ridges.

A Deafening Hug

Mitzie's collar jingled when her mistress
Lay back in her old mahogany rocking chair.
The bells released a quick crisp ringing note
Each time the undulating swaying creaked.

The companion gazing, twilights squeezed
Into the corners, the ceiling above greyed
And wrinkled. Through the cobwebbed window
The autumn's afternoon sun gently waved

His smoked wand. Around the chubby neck
The choke jingled again – a deafening hug.

The Journey

Dislodged from the rain-stained crinkled curtain
A motionless moth landed on the floor when the fan
Rattled. Thumping quickened, the rosewood divan
Creaked, and the mid-air turbulence swelled.

The hollow shell took off and swung round and round
Dashing every corner of the deserted meeting hall
– A drunken sepoy staggering, finally tumbling down
On his head over the edge of the large satin bolster.

The log lying puffing, prompted the fumbled journey
Through the long narrow winding sonorous tunnel.

The Amazing Grace

Caught in the crack of a fallen slab, a tuft of wig's hair
Shakes wryly in the summer breeze, the morning amber
Dripping through the Rastafarian locks over the singer's
Long tickling limbs reaching for the guitar. Admirers

Gather around. And comes Johnny boy in hunting boots
With his dog: a whip in one hand, a hi in the other, a Havana
Between lips, the Stetson flicking the hunchback heaven
Further up. Startled by the amazing grace, the master

And the companion collapse on their backs like the twin
Towers three seasons ago – the crumbled cigar still burning.

Fraternity Meal

No scratching by bare nails, no digging or ploughing
By shaped spears, it's patting and licking by a flaming
Serpentine tongue for a sumptuous global fraternity.
The burden earth brings fast savouries to the table

For celebration. Everyday is a feast: dishes adorned
With aromas and colours; ingredients finest, instant,
Organic; greens, fibres; smoothly blended, seasoned, and
Flavoured – the real nitty-gritty considered meticulously.

No tickling, no tingling, the mannequin springs to tell
The thrilling saga of being cooked to entice delicate tongues.

The Grand Wushi Ware

The grand Wushi ware cannot hold her any more:
Bunches of blinking buds in palms, limbs raised
Skyward, the cactus crouched in the cushioned
Divan, thorns scratching backs of bouncing bees.

Washed in rain the robust feet stick out their long
Rubbery toes through the cracks of the round wall.
An abandoned kitten joins the ants' horde to steal
The grace the noble guest has been enjoying so long.

The pot's purple skin peels off, a hag hanging loose
Sinking into the earth in the mansion's backyard.

The Gecko

The little ticking gecko has already mastered the crafty art
Of staying calm – a slick baby-faced house lizard
Frescoed in beige under the ceiling, tail featured in full,
Eyes set upon a huge moth in rust jacket on the wall.

The sky below is about to lose the last star when
The dreamer turned side in his bed. Heavily sweating,
He fumbles miserably to shut the timepiece babbling
In delirium. A tug at the robe stops him blinking:

Sticking out her wet tongue the huntress comes closer
– The stained crinkled jacket dumped on the damp floor.

A Slight Tremor

A slight tremor in the neighbouring Timor Sea
Made the purple mound crack, dust sliding fast
Down the bulging cheeks, stammer prolonged
Shuffling into a long saga of yester-millennia

When the sky was not far away and the feather quilted
Moon was home of the young bride. Her visit in the night
Lifted the valley to the plateau, hands waved in glee
Like tinsel, veil trailing like a fluttering bark sail.

And the message sticks from the ancestors
Were brought by the swift feet shooting stars.

The Haze

Devoid of ripples, the winter's thickened milky haze
Advances to the land with the gait of a saintly egret:
The succulent bellies of Bombay ducks lying flat
On hot sands – the stench oozing from the gruelling

Turnaround from thrilling sports to meeting mates
In bundles, the small wings hovering above, dropping
Notes of adulation, and the big wings waiting – eyes
Binoculared from the treetops along the edge.

Trucks will soon arrive puffing out choking smoke
Branding all marks of sweating on the busy beach.

Peace

Peace is not word or slogan
Peace is not an expo or world cup
Peace is not humming or opera
Peace is not symphony on a stage

Peace is joining hands
Peace is sitting around a table
Peace is a baby in a safe crib
Peace is a mother by the side

Peace is rain on thirsty sands
Peace is a morsel for the hungry.

Bali 2002

Drenched in a heavy shower of hot ash
The child came running, utterly panicked
For he heard his uncle's frantic plea
From the Sari Club: Please stay inside.

Stay with your dearest ones for safety.
Are you inside home to save your life, Dad?
The whole street is out there in puzzlement:
What the hell is going on in the Jalan Legian?

*

The club and another bar just collapsed
Falling flat to the ground
Puffing out huge lumps of ash
As hot as fire balls

I've never seen such a thing
In my life, Dad – not even
In a great cowboy picture, so much
Smoke gushing out like hell

*

Handing out a cuppa to the lady in a wheelchair
Dad assured the boy: when lightning strikes a tree
The remaining branch still blooms to thrill us
When a cliff collapses the valley grows shrubs

When tsunamis hit shores women pick greens
In the submerged gardens to feed their babies
When clouds don't pour rain for years and years
Camels go out on their trails pulling caravans.

*

We're closest to nature
When we share our warmth
With those who shiver
In sheer coldness.

It's awakening to this call
That keeps our fire burning.
Have a glass of milk, dear
We'll talk about smoke later.

The Caterpillar

Sliding under the quilt of fluffy curly swamp leaves
The caterpillar soon sticks out his tired dirt-smeared
Head in utter desperation to feel the night's dews -
For the earth is a bundle of damn dull dried up skin

Tightly tied with a million-moon-long clumsy sisal twine
Chewed up by screeching wheels of seasons' crazy whims:
Rooted star-studded gazes conquering only other cracks,
Hovering meteors hitting only abandoned memorabilia.

The crawling feet will never scratch even his belly
To relieve fatigue or for an enticing dance pose.

Kunabibi

Mounds of sands are galleried up
Like rock-cut busts, guarding
Sparks of rapturous words
In their punctured hearts:

A yarn of enormous girth
Zigzagging across the land
Lying in deep waterholes
Spanning the two spheres.

*

As the tail moves
The earth springs to life,
As the arrows leave the eyes
The fireball dangles from above.

As the hot winds pass by
The signs suffocate –
The crumbles pile up
Witnessing the track just trodden.

The Arc

The new shoot of dawn's amber
Trots in cool ivory glow:
The trail meandering across the valley,
Crickets resonating in thick shrubs -

The earth's fragrance devoured bare
By the troupes of croaking toads,
Buds nipped by the roaring thrusts
In the monsoon's deep blue mighty nights.

The face pecked all over by the summer's
Blazing tongs, the tickles under feet
Drill through the terrain's dumb walls
To let the laughter burst into pearls.

The meticulously carved bust
Sits on the arc's one end,
The tiny toes between the quilt's folds
Hitting the other for a swing.

The Summit

Those not shivering a bit
In the bizarre biting blizzard
On the treacherous trail
To the cliff-top tower

Had their fettered feet
Freed forever
Cords snapped off
From their anchors

Those not stumbling
On the steep slippery rocks
Had their ribcages
Ballooned to pull them up

Arms fondly hugging
Deep warm breath
Of their lifelong mates
Left behind on the steps

Those not looking back
Over the trodden slopes
Down the terrain
Had their gaze fixed

On the tower's dome
Gracing the summit
To keep their burning quest
Pinned to their bosoms.

*

Those not resonating
Their favourite chants
Had their vibrant lines
Neatly embroidered

With hooked needles
On spreads of silk
Tucked into their
Wriggling spines

The words were steaming hot
To wake up mummies
From their eon-long
Mouldy slumber

The maze of colours
Beaming dazzling plumes
Of dancing peacocks
Before their glassy eyes

Cascading down a flame tree
The scroll fluttered
To let them go
From their stuffy chambers

Over the open fields
Beyond the dunes
Beyond the valleys
Beyond the seas

*

Those not drumming
At deaf ears
Not beating chests
Before frozen faces

Had their air vented
Every corner
Presence stretched
Beyond horizons

Those not making signs
Not humming melodies
Not despatching doves
With bold festoons

Had their warm hands touched
The grips behind the shields
Switched on lights in the trenches
Whispered peace into their bones

Those not bustling anymore
Had dug out their stuff bare
To bring tranquillity
And cool to the marrow

A sprinkle of pearly pats
Over grey sands
A spark of thrilling rapture
Over fractured limbs

*

On the long white beach
Where kin and neighbours
And visitors from the ranches
Gathered in a frenzy

The children screamed
'Have they gone, gone forever?'
The echo returned
And promptly tattooed

On their wiggly backs
With blow paint
In dark waxy
Bubbly blobs

'We are here, we are with you.'
Then the charred souls
Waving their hands
Set off for the cliff-top tower

That was in smoko time
Last fall at Manhattan
When the lotus bloomed
In the heart-shaped lake

Not far away
From the other towers
Sprinkling hot ashes over the trail
To the summit's dome.

About the Author

Prithvindra Chakravarti's earlier poems and trans-creations have been published in Papua Pocket Pockets (Port Moresby) and Writers Workshop series (Kolkata). His plays and poems recently published in Bengali include *Hanumaanjir Kripaa* (a one-act play, Natyapanji, Kolkata, 2005), *Indur Puraan* (a skit in verse, Natyapanji, Kolkata, 2006) and *Hanser Chhaa Baker Chhaa* (poems, Papyrus, Kolkata, 2008). He currently lives in Adelaide.

www.ingramcontent.com/pod-product-compliance
Lightning Source LLC
Chambersburg PA
CBHW062153100526
44589CB00014B/1816